POWER OF CREATIVE MINDS

EXPLORING THE ART AND SCIENCE OF CREATIVE THINKING

SUDHAKAR RAJ

Contents

Introduction

Have you ever been in awe of a great work of art, marvelled at an ingenious invention, or been inspired by a ground-breaking idea? These are all products of creative minds at work. Creativity is a fundamental human trait that has been celebrated throughout history, from ancient cave paintings to modern-day technological innovations.

But what is it that sets creative minds apart? What allows some individuals to consistently generate innovative and imaginative ideas while others struggle to think outside the box? The answer lies in the way that creative minds approach the world around them.

This book is a journey through the minds of some of the most creative individuals in history, exploring their unique thought processes and examining the ways in which they have harnessed their creativity to achieve remarkable success. From artists and musicians to scientists and entrepreneurs, we will delve into the inner workings of some of the world's most innovative minds and uncover the secrets of their success.

But this book is not just a tribute to the accomplishments of others. It is a call to action for readers to tap into their own creative potential and unleash the power of their minds. Throughout the pages of this book, you will be challenged to examine your own ways of thinking and encouraged to explore new approaches to problem-solving, idea generation, and self-expression.

So let's begin the journey into world of creative minds, and discover how you too can unleash the power of your own imagination.

What is Creative Thinking

Creative thinking is the process of generating unique, innovative, and imaginative ideas or solutions to problems. It involves breaking away from conventional or traditional ways of thinking and approaching a problem or situation with an open mind, curiosity and willingness to take risks by divergent thinking.

Creative thinking often involves combining seemingly unrelated concepts or ideas to come up with something new and original.

Creative thinking can be applied to a wide range of fields, including the arts, sciences, business, and daily life. It is not limited to a specific set of skills or talents, and anyone can learn to be more creative by adopting certain attitudes and practices.

Some common characteristics of creative thinkers include the ability to think outside the box, a willingness to experiment and take risks, an openness to new ideas and perspectives, and a strong sense of curiosity and imagination. Creative thinking is a

valuable skill that

Why Creative Thinking matters

Creative thinking is important for several reasons:

Solving problems: Creative thinking helps individuals to solve problems by generating unique and innovative solutions. It allows individuals to think outside the box and approach problems from a new angle.

Innovation: Creative thinking is critical for innovation. Innovation is the process of developing new ideas or improving existing ones to create value. It requires individuals to think creatively to develop new and unique products, services, or processes.

Adaptability: In today's rapidly changing world, adaptability is crucial. Creative thinking helps individuals to adapt to changing circumstances by enabling them to come up with new and innovative ideas.

Personal growth: Engaging in creative thinking can lead to personal growth. It can expand an individual's perspective, increase self-awareness, and enhance problem-solving skills.

Career success: Creative thinking is highly valued by employers as it helps individuals to develop new ideas, innovate, and solve complex problems. Creative thinkers are often sought after for leadership positions as they can drive innovation and growth within an organization.

Role of Brain in Creative Thinking

The brain plays a crucial role in creative thinking. Creative thinking is a complex cognitive process that involves generating new ideas, making connections between seemingly unrelated concepts, and coming up with innovative solutions to problems.

The brain's prefrontal cortex is involved in creative thinking, which is responsible for higher-order cognitive processes, such as planning, decision-making, and problem-solving. The prefrontal cortex is also involved in working memory, which is essential for retaining information while actively manipulating it.

The brain's right hemisphere is often associated with creative thinking, as it is involved in processing visual and spatial information, as well as recognizing patterns and making connections between seemingly unrelated concepts. The right hemisphere also plays a role in processing emotions and feelings, which can be important in creative thinking.

Additionally, various brain networks, such as the default mode network, have been linked to creative thinking. The default mode network is a set of brain regions that become active when the mind is at rest, and it is thought to be involved in processes such as self-reflection, memory consolidation, and creative thinking.

The brain is a complex and multifaceted organ that plays a critical role in creative thinking. A better understanding of the neural mechanisms underlying creative thinking can lead to new insights into how we can enhance our creativity and problem-solving abilities.

Interesting Facts About Brain

Here are some interesting and powerful facts about the brain:

- The human brain weighs around 3 pounds (1.4 kilograms) and is composed of approximately 100 billion neurons.

- The brain is the most energy-hungry organ in the body, accounting for about 20% of the body's energy expenditure.

- The left and right hemispheres of the brain have different functions. The left hemisphere is associated with logical and analytical thinking, while the right hemisphere is associated with creativity and intuition.

- The brain is capable of processing information at an incredible speed. It can process visual information in as little as 13 milliseconds.

- The brain is constantly changing and adapting to new experiences. This ability is known as neuroplasticity.

- The brain contains a complex network of blood vessels that supply it with oxygen and nutrients. If these blood vessels become damaged, it can lead to cognitive impairment and other neurological disorders.

- The brain is responsible for producing and regulating a wide range of hormones, which can influence mood, behaviour, and many other physiological functions.

- The human brain is one of the most complex structures in the known universe, with an estimated 100 trillion connections between neurons.

- The brain can generate enough electricity to power a small light bulb, with the average brain producing around 10 watts of power.

- The brain is capable of rewiring itself in response to injury or disease. This can lead to remarkable recoveries in some cases, such as in patients who have suffered strokes or traumatic brain injuries.

Phineas Gag- An Important milestone in Neuroscience

In 1848, Gage was working as a railroad construction foreman in Vermont. He was using an iron tamping rod to pack explosive powder into a hole when an accidental explosion sent the rod through his left cheek, through his brain, and out the top of his skull.

Remarkably, Gage was conscious and able to speak immediately after the accident, but his personality and behaviour underwent significant changes. Prior to the accident, Gage was described as a responsible, dependable, and hard-working individual. However, after the accident, he became impulsive, indecisive, and unreliable. He was unable to hold down a job and became a drifter, eventually passing away from seizures in 1860.

The case of Phineas Gage is significant because it provided early evidence of the link between brain damage and personality changes. Gage's injury damaged his prefrontal cortex, a region of the brain that is crucial for decision-making, planning, and impulse control. Gage's personality changes were attributed to damage to this region of his brain, highlighting the critical role of the prefrontal cortex in regulating behaviour and personality.

The case of Phineas Gage also led to increased interest in the study of neuroscience and helped researchers better understand the relationship between brain function and behaviour. Today, Gage's story is still studied and discussed in psychology and neuroscience courses around the world.

(There are books specifically devoted to Phineas Gage that you can explore if you would like to delve further into this case.)

Critical vs Creative Thinking

Though this book is focused on Creative thinking, it is important to understand about Critical thinking as well.

Critical thinking and creative thinking are two distinct types of thinking that serve different purposes. Critical thinking involves evaluating and analyzing information to form a judgment or opinion, often through a process of logical reasoning and problem-solving. It involves identifying assumptions, evaluating evidence, and considering multiple perspectives before arriving at a conclusion. Critical thinking is often used in academic, professional, and scientific contexts.

Creative thinking, on the other hand, involves generating new and original ideas, often through a process of brainstorming, free association, and lateral thinking. It involves breaking away from conventional thinking and exploring new and unconventional approaches to problems and challenges. Creative thinking is often used in artistic, entrepreneurial, and innovative contexts.

Both types of thinking are important and valuable in different situations. Critical thinking is useful for evaluating and making sense of complex information, while creative thinking is useful for generating new ideas and approaches. In many cases, a combination of critical and creative thinking can lead to the most effective problem-solving and decision-making outcomes.

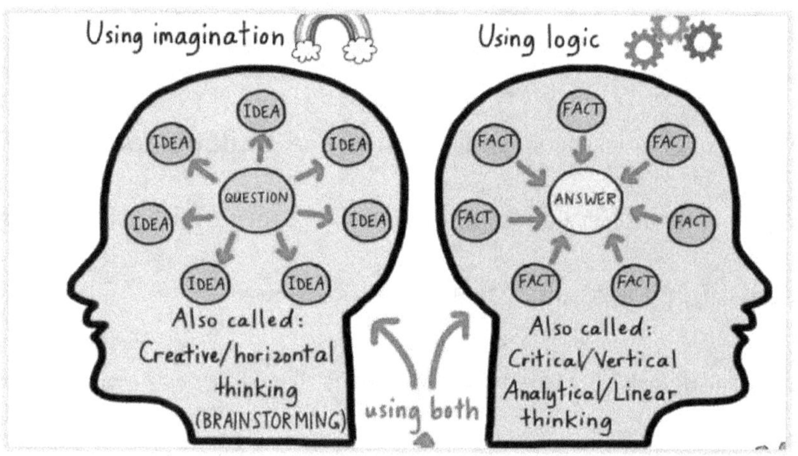

World without Creativity

World without creativity would be a very dull and monotonous place. Creativity is what drives innovation and without it, progress in fields such as art, science, technology and literature would come to a standstill.

In a world without creativity, people would lack the ability to come up with new and original ideas, and everything would be limited to what already exists. There would be no new inventions, no breakthroughs in science or technology, no new forms of artistic expression, and no new literature.

The absence of creativity would also lead to a lack of diversity and individuality, as people would be unable to express themselves in unique and original ways. Society would become stagnant, with little change or evolution. In short, a world without creativity would be a world with limited potential and possibilities.

Now imagine a world without creativity-

How would you read this book if it were not created and accessible?

Think of everything you are using today: your phone, your laptop, your car, your computer, your kitchen, your bed, your television – all created through deep and divergent thinking and outlandish a creative idea.

In the recent COVID pandemic, creativity gained more importance. Creativity was needed to overcome any crisis situation at the earliest and manage it efficiently. We need to think out-of-the box to come up with disruptive ideas that accelerate the transformation of the sectors. Because creativity is not an option instead it's a mandatory tool to redefine our future.

Children's Creative skills

Children's imaginations are often vivid and they are not limited by preconceptions or inhibitions that can stifle creativity in adults. Children are naturally curious, and they are not afraid to take risks or try new things, which are essential qualities for fostering creativity.

Furthermore, research suggests that creative ability is not fixed, but rather can be nurtured and developed over time. This means that children who are encouraged to explore their creativity may develop even stronger creative skills as they grow and mature.

That being said, it's important to note that every child is unique, and not all children will demonstrate the same level of creative ability. Some children may have a natural talent for drawing, painting or other artistic pursuits, while others may excel in other areas, such as music, writing, or problem-solving. The important thing is to provide opportunities for children to explore their interests and express their creativity in ways that are meaningful and fulfilling to them.

Famous Creative Thinkers

History has seen many creative thinkers that changed the world we live today. Their creative thoughts and innovations have contributed to social change and human development.

Some of the notable creative thinkers who were impactful:

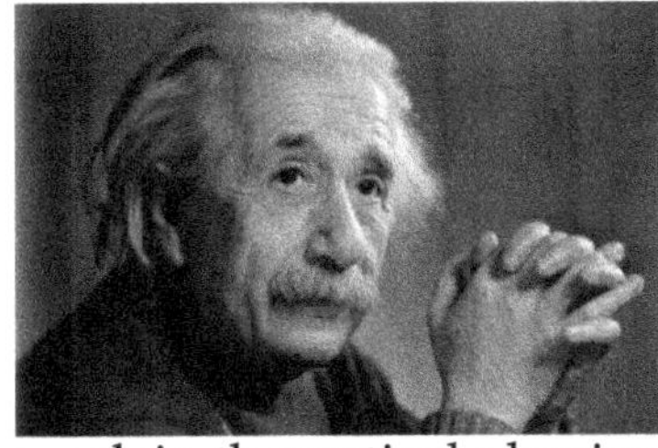

Albert Einstein is often cited as one of the most creative thinkers of the modern era. His ground-breaking work in theoretical physics revolutionized our understanding of the universe and laid the foundation for many of the technological advances we enjoy today.

Einstein's ability to think creatively was influenced by several factors. For one, he had a deep and abiding curiosity about the natural world, and he was constantly questioning established theories and assumptions. He was also unafraid to challenge conventional wisdom and think outside the box, even if it meant going against the prevailing scientific consensus of his time.

Another key aspect of Einstein's creative thinking ability was his willingness to engage in thought experiments, which involved imagining hypothetical scenarios and exploring their implications. By thinking deeply and abstractly about these imaginary scenarios, Einstein was able to develop new and innovative ideas that had eluded other scientists.

Einstein was known for his persistence and perseverance in the face of obstacles and setbacks. He was not easily deterred by failure or disappointment, and he was able to stay focused on his goals and objectives even in the face of significant challenges.

Albert Einstein's creative thinking ability was fueled by a combination of curiosity, imagination, unconventional thinking, and persistence. These qualities helped him to develop ground-breaking new theories and ideas that have had a lasting impact on our understanding of the universe.

Marie Curie was a brilliant scientist who is known for her ground-breaking work in radioactivity and her discovery of the elements radium and polonium. She was not only a skilled and dedicated researcher, but also possessed strong creative thinking abilities that allowed her to make these significant contributions to science.

One aspect of Marie Curie's creative thinking was her ability to approach problems from multiple angles. She was not satisfied with simply accepting conventional explanations, but instead questioned assumptions and sought to understand phenomena in a more nuanced way. This led her to develop new methods for measuring radioactivity, for example, and to challenge the prevailing views on the nature of the atom.

Another aspect of Marie Curie's creative thinking was her willingness to take risks and pursue unconventional ideas. She was not afraid to challenge established beliefs and take on projects that were considered too difficult or too speculative by others. Her persistence and determination in the face of these challenges helped her to make ground-breaking discoveries that revolutionized our understanding of the natural world.

Marie Curie's creative thinking abilities were essential to her success as a scientist. Her willingness to think outside the box, question assumptions, and take risks allowed her to make significant contributions to the field of radioactivity and to inspire generations of scientists to come.

 **Charles Darwin** was known for his ground-breaking scientific work in the theory of evolution, which he developed over many years of observation and experimentation. He is considered to be one of the most influential scientists of all time, and his work has had a profound impact on our understanding of the natural world.

Darwin's ability to think creatively was central to his success as a scientist. He was a keen observer of the natural world, and he was able to make connections between different phenomena that others had not noticed before. He also had the ability to think outside the box and challenge conventional wisdom, which allowed him to develop a new and revolutionary theory of evolution.

In addition to his creative thinking abilities, Darwin was also a dedicated and persistent researcher. He spent many years studying the natural world and collecting data to support his ideas, and he was not deterred by the criticism and opposition he faced from others.

Charles Darwin's creative thinking ability was a key factor in his success as a scientist. His ability to think critically, observe the natural world, and challenge conventional wisdom allowed him to develop a new and ground-breaking theory of evolution that has stood the test of time.

Creativities that changed the World

Throughout history, there have been countless creative individuals whose ideas and inventions have had a profound impact on the world. From advancements in technology and medicine to breakthroughs in the arts and sciences, these creativities have changed the course of history and shaped the world we live in today.

My top pick would be the invention of aircraft. The aircraft is considered one of the greatest inventions of all time due to the incredible impact it has had on society and the world as a whole.

The Wright Brothers, Orville and Wilbur, are credited with inventing and building the world's first successful airplane. Their achievement was a result of a combination of creativity, persistence, and innovation.

One of the key elements of the Wright Brothers' success was their ability to think creatively about the problem of flight. They studied the flight of birds and observed how they used their wings to maintain stability and maneuver in the air. From this, they developed a new concept of controlling an aircraft that involved a system of wing warping that allowed the pilot to steer the plane.

The Wright Brothers also built their own wind tunnel to test the aerodynamics of their designs, which was an innovative approach at the time. They conducted a series of experiments to refine their designs and test their theories, which ultimately led to the successful flight of their airplane.

Furthermore, the Wright Brothers were persistent in their efforts to achieve flight. They faced numerous setbacks and challenges along the way, but they continued to work tirelessly to overcome these obstacles and refine their designs. They were also willing to take risks and push the boundaries of what was possible, which ultimately led to their success.

Wright Brothers' creative thinking, persistence, and innovation were critical in their invention of the first successful airplane. Their willingness to challenge conventional wisdom and pursue a new and innovative approach to flight changed the course of history and opened-up a whole new world of possibilities for human travel and transportation.

Psychology of Creativity

The psychology of creativity is a field of study that seeks to understand how and why creative ideas are generated and developed. Creativity is a complex phenomenon that involves many different cognitive processes, and researchers in this field aim to identify the key factors that contribute to creative thinking.

One important aspect of the psychology of creativity is the role of divergent thinking, which is the ability to generate a wide range of ideas and possibilities. This type of thinking is often associated with creativity, as it allows individuals to explore different perspectives and come up with novel solutions to problems.

Another important factor in the psychology of creativity is the influence of various cognitive processes such as attention, memory, and perception. For example, research has shown that individuals who are able to sustain their attention for long periods of time may be more likely to generate creative ideas, as they are better able to focus on and explore different possibilities.

Personality traits are also thought to play a role in creativity. For example, individuals who are open to new experiences, willing to take risks, and able to tolerate ambiguity may be more likely to generate creative ideas.

The environment and context in which creative thinking takes place can also play a role in the psychology of creativity. Factors such as social norms, cultural expectations, and the physical environment can all influence the types of ideas and solutions that are generated.

Psychology of creativity is a complex and multidimensional field that seeks to understand the many factors that contribute to creative thinking. By better understanding the psychology of creativity, researchers and practitioners can help to foster and promote creative thinking in individuals and organizations.

In the past, scientists thought that creativity came solely from the right hemisphere of the brain, but more recent discoveries have shown that many neural networks across the brain spark creativity and control our responses to various stimuli.

Creativity is defined by noted psychologist John R. Hayes as, "the potential of persons to produce creative works whether or not they have produced any work as yet."

In recent years, scientific evidence has revealed that mental cognition results from the dynamic interactions of distributed brain areas operating in what's called large-scale neural networks.

When we tell a joke or a story or even think about that school days, our brains are taking input from the world around them, accessing memories and creating new thoughts — in short, cognition, the constant of our experience.

Here's a look at three large-scale neural networks that contribute to the psychology of creativity.

Salience Network

The salience network is "an intrinsically connected large-scale network" located deep in the brain within the anterior insula and dorsal anterior cingulate cortex. Studies have found that the salience network contributes to an array of complex brain functions, including social behaviour, communication and self-awareness.

A Stanford University neurologist Michael Greicius and a fellow scientist William Seeley described the salience network as the system that prepares the brain for action. Think of how the brain responds to "fight or flight" stimuli. One example of this is how a driver responds when he or she sees a pedestrian dart across a busy street, or when a person attempts to recall facts quickly during a quiz or trivia game.

In order to make a situation salient, it requires significance to the individual involved. The stimuli for the salient network can come internally, such as feelings of hunger and pain, or from external sources, such as a police siren. As something becomes discernible – as a police car with its sirens blaring becomes louder – the brain is directed to respond. If the stimuli remained far away, we may have been less likely to respond.

In a recent study, Greicius found strong direct evidence that the salience network plays a key role in "motivation and a readiness to act." Interestingly, some individuals with more activity than normal in the salience network have been linked with autism, and some individuals with damage to key areas of the salience network have been diagnosed with a type of dementia.

Tests on lab animals have shown that when the salience network is blocked or interfered with, the animals gave up more easily when trying to find food through a maze than those whose salience network wasn't inhibited.

In all, the salience network helps our brain take in and monitor information from internal or external sources while being flexible enough to give us different stimuli on how to respond to the situations, allowing for creativity in a stressful situation.

Default Mode Network

Even when the brain isn't focused on a particular activity, parts of the brain are functioning at a high level.

Over the past few decades, scientists have been studying the default mode network, a large-scale network of multiple areas of the brain that light up while we are in our resting state, or default mode.

Some of the activities people may be doing when the default mode network is firing through its synapses include daydreaming, recalling memories, and just overall thinking about different subjects. According to Randy Buckner, the default mode network is involved with "constructing dynamic mental simulations based on personal past experiences such as used during remembering, thinking about the future, and generally when imagining alternative perspectives and scenarios to the present." The default mode network is also involved in social cognition.

Studies have shown that disruption to the default mode network has been linked with natural aging and brain diseases such as Alzheimer's disease.

It should be noted that some in the psychology community disagree that there is a default mode network, as it is difficult to define exactly what is resting state compared to others.

Executive Attention Network

The executive attention network is a large-scale network that monitors and resolves conflict between thoughts, feelings and responses.

Executive attention is the ability for the mind to focus on one thing and block out the distractions, which is an important skill for children to learn. The executive attention network lights up when concentrating on a difficult test or engaging in a challenging problem-solving activity. The network is located "across the lateral (outer) regions of the prefrontal cortex and areas toward the back (posterior) of the parietal lobe."

The executive attention network deals with working memory (short-term and application of long-term memory to the present) and the following tasks of thought: planning, switching and inhibition.

Types of Creativity

There are several types of creativity, each of which involves different ways of thinking and generating new ideas. Here are a few examples:

Artistic Creativity: Artistic creativity involves the ability to produce original and imaginative works of art, such as paintings, sculptures, music, and literature. This type of creativity often relies on intuitive and subjective thinking, and may be inspired by emotions, feelings, and personal experiences.

Scientific Creativity: Scientific creativity involves the ability to generate new ideas and discoveries in science and technology. This type of creativity often relies on analytical and logical thinking, and may involve experimentation, observation, and problem-solving.

Social Creativity: Social creativity involves the ability to generate new ideas and solutions to social problems, such as poverty, inequality, and conflict. This type of creativity often involves collaboration and communication and may be driven by a desire to create positive change in the world.

Entrepreneurial Creativity: Entrepreneurial creativity involves the ability to generate new ideas and solutions for starting and growing businesses. This type of creativity often involves risk-taking, innovation, and strategic thinking, and may be driven by a desire to create value and make a profit.

Personal Creativity: Personal creativity involves the ability to generate new ideas and solutions for personal growth and development, such as self-improvement, learning, and self-expression. This type of creativity may be inspired by personal goals, interests, and passions, and may involve experimentation, reflection, and self-discovery.

The different types of creativity highlight the diverse ways in which people can generate new ideas and solutions and emphasize the importance of creativity in a wide range of domains and contexts.

Stages of the Creative Process

The creative process can be broken down into several stages that individuals typically go through when generating new ideas and developing them into a final product. Here are the common stages of the creative process:

Preparation: This stage involves gathering information, exploring different perspectives, and identifying the problem or challenge to be addressed. It is important to have a clear understanding of the goals and objectives of the creative endeavour before moving on to the next stage.

Incubation: In this stage, the individual allows the problem or challenge to "incubate" in their mind, and takes a break from actively thinking about it. This allows the subconscious mind to work on the problem in the background and can lead to new insights and ideas.

Insight: The insight stage involves a sudden realization or "aha moment" when the individual comes up with a new and innovative idea. This stage may be preceded by a period of frustration or confusion, as the individual struggles to find a solution to the problem.

Evaluation: This stage involves critically evaluating the new idea and determining whether it is feasible and appropriate for the given problem or challenge. This stage may also involve identifying potential obstacles or limitations and developing strategies for overcoming them.

Elaboration: In this stage, the individual develops the new idea into a more concrete and detailed plan, often through further research and experimentation. This stage may also involve refining the idea and making adjustments based on feedback from others.

Implementation: The final stage of the creative process involves actually bringing the idea to life, whether through artistic expression, scientific experimentation, or other means. This stage may involve collaboration with others, problem-solving, and adapting to unexpected challenges.

The creative process can be a highly iterative and non-linear process, with individuals moving back and forth between different stages as they refine and develop their ideas. The key is to remain open to new insights and ideas, and to be persistent in pursuing the creative vision.

Common obstacles to Creativity and how to overcome

While creativity can be an incredibly rewarding and fulfilling experience, it is not always easy to access. There are many common obstacles that can get in the way of creative thinking, including:

Fear of failure: Many people are hesitant to take risks and try new things for fear of failure or rejection. This can lead to a lack of creativity, as individuals may be unwilling to explore new ideas or take on challenges.

Self-doubt: Some individuals may struggle with self-doubt or negative self-talk that can limit their creative potential. They may feel that their ideas are not good enough or that they do not have the skills or knowledge to pursue them.

Lack of inspiration: Sometimes, individuals may feel stuck or uninspired, and may struggle to generate new ideas or solutions.

Overthinking: Overthinking or analyzing a problem too much can lead to a lack of creativity, as individuals may become stuck in their own thoughts and unable to see things from different perspectives.

Distractions: In today's fast-paced world, it can be difficult to find the time and space for creative thinking, as there are many distractions and competing demands for attention.

To overcome these obstacles and unlock your creativity, here are some strategies you can try:

Embrace failure: Rather than fearing failure, try to see it as an opportunity for learning and growth. Accept that not every idea will be successful and use feedback and critique as a way to improve.

Practice positive self-talk: Challenge negative self-talk and focus on positive affirmations that can help build confidence and self-belief.

Seek out new experiences: Expose yourself to new experiences, people, and ideas. This can help broaden your perspective and stimulate new ways of thinking.

Practice mindfulness: Mindfulness techniques such as meditation or deep breathing can help quiet the mind and reduce overthinking, allowing for more free-flowing creative thinking.

Create a dedicated creative space: Set aside time and space for creative thinking, free from distractions and interruptions. This can help create a conducive environment for generating new ideas and solutions.

The key to overcoming obstacles to creativity is to remain open, curious, and persistent, and to try new strategies until you find what works for you.

Techniques to enhance Creativity

Creativity is the ability to come up with new and innovative ideas and solutions to problems. Here are some techniques that can help enhance creativity:

Brainstorming: Brainstorming is a technique used to generate a large number of ideas in a short period of time. This technique encourages people to think outside the box and come up with as many ideas as possible, without judging or evaluating them. This technique can be done alone or in a group.

Mind Mapping: Mind mapping is a visual technique that can be used to generate and organize ideas. This technique involves drawing a diagram that connects different ideas and concepts, allowing the brain to make new connections and associations between different ideas.

Taking breaks: Taking breaks and allowing the mind to rest can help stimulate creativity. Stepping away from a problem or project and engaging in a different activity can help to recharge the brain and approach the problem from a different angle.

Collaborating: Collaborating with others can help to enhance creativity by bringing different perspectives and ideas to the table. When people work together, they can bounce ideas off each other and come up with new solutions that may not have been possible otherwise.

Changing your routine: Changing your routine can help to stimulate creativity. Doing things differently, such as taking a different route to work or trying a new hobby, can help to break out of old patterns and generate new ideas.

Engaging in creative activities: Engaging in creative activities, such as painting, writing or playing music, can help to stimulate creativity in other areas of life. These activities allow the mind to be free and explore new ideas and possibilities.

Setting goals: Setting goals and deadlines can help to focus the mind and provide a framework for generating new ideas. By setting a goal, the mind is forced to think creatively in order to achieve the desired outcome.

Cultivating a Creative Mindset

Cultivating a creative mindset is essential for those looking to innovate, problem-solve, and create new ideas. Creativity is not just reserved for artists and designers, but it can be applied to all aspects of life, from business to personal development. Here are some tips for cultivating a creative mindset:

Embrace curiosity: Curiosity is the starting point of creativity. By asking questions, exploring new ideas, and seeking to understand the world around us, we can start to think more creatively. Embracing curiosity means being open-minded and willing to challenge assumptions.

Practice mindfulness: Mindfulness is the practice of being present in the moment and paying attention to one's thoughts and feelings. This practice can help to cultivate a creative mindset by increasing awareness and focus. By practicing mindfulness, one can learn to let go of distractions and negative thoughts that may stifle creativity.

Be willing to take risks: Creativity often requires taking risks and stepping outside of one's comfort zone. It is important to be willing to try new things, even if they may not work out. Failure is a natural part of the creative process and should be embraced as a learning opportunity.

Find inspiration in everyday life: Inspiration can come from anywhere, and it is important to be open to new experiences and ideas. Paying attention to the world around us and seeking inspiration in everyday life can help to stimulate creativity.

Surround yourself with creativity: Surrounding yourself with creative people and environments can help to foster a creative mindset. This may mean attending art exhibits, taking a creative writing class, or joining a brainstorming session.

Embrace ambiguity: Ambiguity can be uncomfortable, but it is often a necessary part of the creative process. Being comfortable with uncertainty and embracing ambiguity can help to generate new ideas and solutions.

Practice divergent thinking: Divergent thinking is the process of generating multiple ideas and solutions. This can be practiced by brainstorming, mind mapping, and other techniques that encourage idea generation. By practicing divergent thinking, one can expand their thinking and explore new possibilities.

Cultivating a creative mindset is not a one-time event, but a continuous practice. By embracing curiosity, taking risks, finding inspiration, and practicing divergent thinking, one can develop a creative mindset that will benefit all aspects of life.

Mindfulness and Creative thinking

Mindfulness is the practice of being present in the moment, paying attention to one's thoughts and feelings without judgment. Creative thinking involves generating new ideas and solutions, often by breaking free from traditional patterns of thought. While mindfulness and creative thinking may seem like opposing concepts, they can actually complement each other.

Practicing mindfulness can help to quiet the mind and reduce distractions, allowing space for creative thinking to emerge. By being present in the moment, one can focus more fully on the task at hand, allowing the mind to explore new ideas and possibilities. Mindfulness can also help to reduce anxiety and stress, which can be barriers to creative thinking.

In addition, mindfulness can help to increase awareness and perception. By paying attention to the world around us, we can notice details and patterns that we may have missed before. This increased awareness can help to generate new ideas and perspectives.

Mindfulness can also help to break free from limiting beliefs and patterns of thought. By practicing non-judgment and acceptance, one can learn to let go of preconceived notions and explore new possibilities. This can lead to more divergent thinking, allowing for a wider range of ideas and solutions.

Mindfulness can help to increase patience and persistence. Creative thinking often involves trial and error, and it can be easy to become discouraged when ideas don't immediately work out. By practicing mindfulness, one can learn to stay focused on the process and maintain a positive attitude, even in the face of setbacks.

Mindfulness and creative thinking can work together to enhance innovation, problem-solving, and personal growth. By cultivating a mindful approach to creative thinking, one can develop a deeper understanding of their own thought processes, increase awareness and perception, and generate new and innovative ideas.

Importance of Curiosity and Experimentation

Curiosity and experimentation are two critical components of innovation, problem-solving, and personal growth. Here are some of the key reasons why they are so important:

Curiosity fuels learning: Curiosity is the desire to learn and understand more about the world around us. It drives us to explore new ideas, ask questions, and seek out new experiences. When we are curious, we are more engaged in the learning process and more likely to retain the information we gather.

Experimentation drives innovation: Experimentation is the process of trying new things and testing out new ideas. By experimenting, we can discover what works and what doesn't, and we can develop new solutions to problems. Without experimentation, we would be limited to existing solutions and ideas, and innovation would be stifled.

Curiosity leads to new ideas: When we are curious, we are more likely to explore new and different ideas. This can lead to the discovery of new solutions, approaches, and opportunities. Curiosity can also help us to identify problems and challenges that we may not have noticed otherwise.

Experimentation leads to progress: Experimentation is the process of trial and error, and it often involves making mistakes and encountering obstacles. However, by persisting through these challenges, we can make progress and develop new skills and knowledge.

Curiosity and experimentation foster creativity: Creativity is the ability to generate new ideas and solutions, often by combining existing concepts in new and innovative ways. Curiosity and experimentation are essential components of creativity, as they allow us to explore new ideas, perspectives, and possibilities.

Curiosity and experimentation are essential for learning, innovation, problem-solving, personal growth, and creativity. By embracing these qualities, we can expand our knowledge and skills, generate new ideas and solutions, and make progress towards our goals.

Embracing failure and learning from mistakes

Not every creative ideas will succeed, so it is important to embrace and learn from such failures.

Failure and mistakes are inevitable parts of life, but they can also be valuable opportunities for learning and growth. Here are some of the key reasons why embracing failure and learning from mistakes is so important:

Failure is a necessary part of the learning process: Learning often involves making mistakes and encountering obstacles. By embracing failure as a necessary part of the learning process, we can adopt a more positive attitude towards our mistakes and use them as opportunities for growth and improvement.

Mistakes can help us identify areas for improvement: When we make mistakes, we can use them as opportunities to identify areas where we can improve. By analyzing our mistakes and identifying what went wrong, we can develop strategies for avoiding similar mistakes in the future.

Failure can lead to new opportunities: Sometimes failure can lead to new and unexpected opportunities. By embracing failure and remaining open to new possibilities, we can discover new solutions, opportunities, and perspectives.

Failure builds resilience: By experiencing failure and overcoming adversity, we can develop resilience and the ability to bounce back from setbacks. This can be a valuable skill in both personal and professional contexts.

Learning from mistakes fosters innovation: Innovation often involves trying new things and taking risks. By learning from our mistakes, we can develop new and innovative solutions to problems, as well as new approaches and perspectives.

Embracing failure and learning from mistakes is an essential part of personal and professional growth. By adopting a growth mindset and using failure as an opportunity for learning and improvement, we can develop resilience, creativity and the ability to overcome obstacles and achieve our goals.

Creativity in the Arts

Creativity is a vital component of artistic expression. The arts, which encompass a wide range of creative endeavors, including visual art, music, literature, theater, and dance, rely heavily on the power of creativity to generate new and innovative works of art.

In the visual arts, creativity can manifest in many ways. It may involve exploring new techniques or materials, experimenting with color and composition, or developing a unique style or aesthetic. Visual artists often use their creativity to express their emotions, ideas, and experiences in a way that is visually compelling and thought-provoking.

Music is another form of art that heavily relies on creativity. Musicians use their creativity to compose and perform original music, often drawing inspiration from a variety of sources, including personal experiences, emotions, and cultural influences. Creativity in music can involve experimenting with different genres, instruments, and musical styles, as well as pushing the boundaries of what is traditionally considered "musical."

Literature, which includes novels, poetry, and other forms of written expression, also relies heavily on creativity. Writers use their creativity to develop characters, plotlines, and themes that are engaging and thought-provoking. Creativity in literature can involve experimenting with different narrative techniques, styles, and genres, as well as exploring new and innovative ways of telling a story.

Theater and dance also require a great deal of creativity. Performers use their creativity to develop new and innovative choreography, explore new forms of expression, and push the boundaries of what is traditionally considered "performance." In theater, creativity can involve developing new scripts, characters, and staging techniques that challenge audience expectations and bring fresh perspectives to the art form.

In all of these artistic disciplines, creativity is essential for generating new and innovative works of art. It allows artists to push beyond the limits of what is traditionally considered "artistic," to explore new ideas and techniques, and to express themselves in a way that is unique and thought-provoking. Whether in the visual arts, music, literature, theater, or dance, creativity is a driving force behind the creation of new works of art that challenge, inspire, and transform us.

Creativity in Science and Technology

Creativity plays a significant role in science and technology, driving innovation and discovery. In these fields, creativity involves thinking outside of the box, generating new and unconventional ideas, and exploring possibilities beyond the established norms. Here are some examples of how creativity is used in science and technology:

Research: Creative thinking is essential to the scientific research process. Researchers must develop new and innovative ways to collect, analyze, and interpret data to generate new knowledge and insights.

Problem-Solving: Creative thinking is also critical to solving problems in science and technology. Researchers and engineers must use creative thinking to develop new solutions to complex challenges, and often collaborate across different fields of study to find the most effective solution.

Invention: Creativity is also a driving force behind invention and innovation. Scientists and technologists often use creative thinking to develop new and unconventional ideas, resulting in groundbreaking inventions such as the internet, the personal computer, and the smartphone.

Design: In technology, creative thinking is essential to the design process. Engineers and designers must use their creativity to develop new and innovative products, ensuring that they are not only functional, but also aesthetically pleasing and user-friendly.

Creativity is a vital component of science and technology, driving innovation, invention, and discovery. In a rapidly changing technological landscape, creative thinking is essential to keep up with emerging trends and push beyond the established boundaries. By fostering a culture of creativity in science and technology, we can continue to drive progress and make a positive impact on the world.

Creativity in Business and Entrepreneurship

Creativity is an essential component of business and entrepreneurship, driving innovation and growth. It enables individuals and companies to generate new and unconventional ideas, explore possibilities beyond the established norms, and create new products, services, and markets. Here are some examples of how creativity is used in business and entrepreneurship:

Innovation: Creative thinking is essential to innovation in business. Entrepreneurs and businesses must use their creativity to develop new products, services, and business models that meet the needs of customers and stay ahead of the competition. Innovation can involve experimenting with new ideas, developing prototypes, and testing new products and services.

Marketing: Creative thinking is also critical to effective marketing. Companies must use creative ideas and strategies to capture the attention of consumers, build brand awareness, and differentiate themselves from competitors. This can involve developing creative advertising campaigns, using social media to connect with customers, and creating engaging content.

Problem-Solving: Creative thinking is also essential to problem-solving in business. Entrepreneurs and businesses must use creative thinking to overcome obstacles and find solutions to complex challenges. This can involve developing new strategies, testing new ideas, and collaborating with others to find the best solution.

Design: Creative thinking is also a critical component of design in business. Entrepreneurs and businesses must use their creativity to develop new products and services that are not only functional, but also aesthetically pleasing and user-friendly. This can involve collaborating with designers and engineers to create innovative and visually appealing products and services.

Entrepreneurship: Creativity is also essential to entrepreneurship. Entrepreneurs must use their creativity to identify unmet needs and develop new products or services to meet those needs. This can involve developing new business models, testing new ideas, and collaborating with others to create new opportunities.

Creativity is a vital component of business and entrepreneurship, driving innovation, growth, and success. By fostering a culture of creativity in business and entrepreneurship, we can continue to drive progress and make a positive impact on the world.

The Power of Collaboration in Creative Endeavours

Collaboration is a powerful tool in creative endeavours, enabling individuals to bring together their diverse perspectives, experiences, and skillsets to generate new and innovative ideas. It enables individuals to work together towards a common goal, leveraging each other's strengths and areas of expertise. Here are some examples of how collaboration can enhance creativity:

Idea Generation: Collaboration can generate new and unconventional ideas that would not have been possible with only one person working alone. Working in a team allows individuals to share ideas, brainstorm together, and build on each other's ideas to generate more creative solutions.

Cross-Disciplinary Approaches: Collaboration allows individuals to work across different disciplines, such as art, science, technology, and business, bringing together diverse perspectives and knowledge. This can lead to new approaches to problem-solving, and the development of innovative products and services.

Critique and Feedback: Collaboration can also provide valuable feedback and constructive criticism, helping individuals to refine their ideas and approaches. This feedback can lead to improvements in the quality of the work and help individuals to grow and develop their skills.

Shared Resources: Collaboration enables individuals to share resources, including expertise, materials, and equipment, which can reduce costs and enable access to resources that may not have been available to individuals working alone.

Increased Motivation: Collaboration can also increase motivation and accountability, as individuals are working towards a common goal and can encourage and support each other throughout the creative process.

Collaboration is a powerful tool in creative endeavours, enabling individuals to generate new and innovative ideas, work across different disciplines, receive feedback, share resources, and increase motivation. By fostering a culture of collaboration, we can continue to drive progress and make a positive impact on the world.

Tips For Working in a Creative Team

Working in a creative team can be both rewarding and challenging. Here are some tips to help you and your team work together effectively to achieve your creative goals:

Set clear goals and expectations: Define clear goals for your project and make sure everyone in the team understands the expectations. This can help to keep everyone focused and motivated and ensure that everyone is working towards the same objective.

Foster open communication: Communication is crucial in a creative team. Encourage open and honest communication, and make sure everyone has a chance to contribute their ideas and feedback. This can help to build trust, improve collaboration, and foster a sense of shared ownership of the project.

Embrace diversity: Creative teams are made up of individuals with different perspectives, backgrounds, and skillsets. Embrace this diversity and use it to your advantage. Encourage team members to share their unique perspectives, experiences, and ideas, and create an environment that values and celebrates diversity.

Encourage experimentation: Creative projects often require a lot of trial and error. Encourage your team members to experiment and take risks. This can help to generate new and innovative ideas, and lead to breakthroughs that would not have been possible without taking risks.

Foster a positive and supportive environment: Creativity thrives in a positive and supportive environment. Encourage your team members to support and encourage each other, and celebrate each other's successes. This can help to build a sense of community and shared purpose, and create a more productive and enjoyable working environment.

Be flexible: Creative projects often require flexibility, as the project scope and goals may change over time. Be open to changes and be willing to adapt to new circumstances. This can help to ensure that the project stays on track, and that the team remains focused on achieving its goals.

By following these tips, you can help to create a more productive, collaborative, and enjoyable working environment for your creative team, and achieve your creative goals.

Creative Thinking in Everyday Life

Creative thinking is not just reserved for artists, inventors, or scientists. It's a crucial skill that can help us in our everyday lives, from problem-solving to decision-making. Here are some ways creative thinking can be applied in our daily lives:

Problem-solving: Creative thinking can help us to find new and innovative solutions to problems we face in our daily lives. Instead of approaching a problem in a traditional or routine way, try thinking outside the box and consider alternative approaches. This can help to come up with more effective and efficient solutions.

Decision-making: Creative thinking can help us to make better decisions. By considering multiple perspectives and analyzing different scenarios, we can arrive at better-informed decisions that are more likely to meet our needs and desires.

Communication: Creative thinking can help us to communicate more effectively with others. By using metaphors, analogies, and storytelling, we can convey our ideas and messages in a more engaging and memorable way.

Time Management: Creative thinking can help us to manage our time more effectively. By prioritizing tasks, breaking them down into smaller parts, and finding innovative ways to complete them, we can accomplish more in less time.

Personal growth: Creative thinking can also help us to grow and develop as individuals. By challenging ourselves to think differently and try new things, we can expand our perspectives, learn new skills, and become more adaptable and resilient.

Creative thinking is a powerful tool that can be applied in many areas of our daily lives. By using creative thinking to approach problems, make decisions, communicate more effectively, manage our time, and grow as individuals, we can lead more fulfilling and productive lives.

Applying Creative Thinking to Personal Growth

Applying creative thinking to personal growth and development can help you to unlock new possibilities and achieve your goals. Here are some ways to use creative thinking to support your personal growth and development:

Identify and challenge limiting beliefs: Limiting beliefs can hold you back from achieving your full potential. By identifying and challenging these beliefs, you can expand your horizons and open up new possibilities. Try to reframe negative self-talk and focus on your strengths and abilities.

Brainstorm new ideas: Creative thinking can help you to generate new ideas and solutions to problems you may face in your personal life. Try brainstorming different approaches and experimenting with new strategies.

Embrace change and uncertainty: Creative thinking can help you to adapt to change and uncertainty. By viewing change as an opportunity for growth, you can approach new situations with a sense of curiosity and openness.

Experiment with new experiences: Creative thinking can help you to explore new experiences and expand your horizons. Try new things, visit new places, and expose yourself to different ideas and perspectives.

Use visualization and imagination: Creative thinking can help you to visualize and imagine what you want to achieve. Visualize yourself succeeding and achieving your goals, and use your imagination to find innovative ways to make those goals a reality.

Applying creative thinking to your personal growth and development can help you to unlock your potential, overcome limiting beliefs, and achieve your goals. By embracing change, experimenting with new experiences, and using visualization and imagination, you can open up new possibilities and create a more fulfilling life.

Patent your Ideas/Inventions

A patent is a form of legal protection granted to an inventor or creator of a new and useful invention, process, or design. Obtaining a patent for a creative idea can be important for several reasons:

Protection of intellectual property: A patent provides the creator with legal protection for their idea, preventing others from making, using, selling, or importing the invention without permission. This protection can be crucial for preventing competitors from stealing or replicating the idea.

Financial gain: A patent can provide the creator with the ability to license or sell their idea, allowing them to monetize their creation and potentially earn a significant return on their investment.

Increased credibility: Having a patent can increase the credibility of the creator and their idea, making it easier to attract investors, partners, or customers. It can demonstrate that the creator has a unique and valuable idea that has been recognized by a government authority.

Encourages Innovation: The patent system encourages innovation and creativity by providing an incentive for inventors and creators to invest time and resources into developing new ideas. The potential for patent protection can motivate individuals and businesses to invest in research and development.

Obtaining a patent for a creative idea can be important for protecting intellectual property, providing financial gain, increasing credibility, and encouraging innovation. However, the patent process can be complex and requires significant resources, including time and money. It's important to carefully consider the potential benefits and drawbacks of obtaining a patent and seek professional advice to navigate the process.

<h1 style="text-align:center">Conclusion</h1>

In conclusion, creative thinking is a powerful tool that can be used to solve problems, generate new ideas, and drive innovation in virtually every area of life. Through this book on creative thinking, we have explored various techniques and strategies that can help you tap into your innate creativity and unleash your full potential.

We have discussed the importance of mindset, curiosity, experimentation, and collaboration, and explored how these factors can be leveraged to overcome obstacles and find creative solutions to challenges. We have also examined the application of creative thinking in various fields, including the arts, sciences, business, and personal growth.

By incorporating these strategies and techniques into your everyday life, you can become a more effective problem solver, a more innovative thinker, and a more creative and fulfilled individual. With practice and perseverance, you can develop a more expansive and flexible mindset that is better equipped to handle the challenges and opportunities that come your way.

The journey of creative thinking is one that requires commitment, courage, and an unwavering belief in your ability to create and innovate. This book has provided a roadmap to help you along this journey, but the true key to success lies in your willingness to take risks, challenge assumptions, and embrace the unknown. With this in mind, I encourage you to embark on your own journey of creative thinking and unlock the limitless possibilities that lie ahead.

Lets be Creative and Create a better Tomorrow!

~ Thank You ~

About the Author

Sudhakar Raj is a leadership coach, author and entrepreneur with over 22 years of Industry experience. Conducted several trainings and coached hundreds of people on leadership and other soft skills. Sudhakar worked in top MNCs across the globe like Microsoft Corporation and Deloitte Consulting. Founder of **InnovTelligent Consulting**. Holds an MBA in Finance and IT. Master degree in Economics. Passionate in building great leaders to take on challenges of tomorrow.

Contact him at *sudhakarraj@hotmail.com*